It Is a

By Liza Charlesworth

ISBN: 978-1-339-02662-6

Art Director: Tannaz Fassihi; Designer: Tanya Chernyak
Photos © Getty Images.
Copyright © Liza Charlesworth. All rights reserved. Published by Scholastic Inc.

3 4 5 6 7 8 9 10   68   32 31 30 29 28 27 26 25 24

Printed in Jiaxing, China. First printing, August 2023.

It is a pig.

A pig can sit.

A pig can zip.

A pig can dig in a mud pit.
Ick!

A pig can be big, big, big!

A pig can have six pig kids.

A kid can get a pig.
Pat, pat, pat!

Pig, pig, pig!
Pigs can be pets.